What Children Need to Know When Parents Get Divorced

Books by William Coleman
from Bethany House Publishers

DEVOTIONALS FOR YOUNG CHILDREN
> Fins, Feathers, and Faith
> What Children Need to Know When Parents Get Divorced

DEVOTIONALS FOR TEENS
> Earning Your Wings
> Friends Forever

BOOKS FOR ADULTS
> Before I Give You Away
> Before Your Baby Comes (with Patricia Coleman)
> If I Could Raise My Kids Again
> It's Been a Good Year
> What Makes Your Teen Tick?

What Children

Need to Know

When Parents

Get Divorced

WILLIAM L.
COLEMAN

BETHANY HOUSE PUBLISHERS
MINNEAPOLIS, MINNESOTA 55438

Published by Bethany House Publishers
A Ministry of Bethany Fellowship International
11400 Hampshire Avenue South
Minneapolis, Minnesota 55438
www.bethanyhouse.com

Printed in the United States of America by
Bethany Press International, Minneapolis, Minnesota 55438

Library of Congress Cataloging-in-Publication Data

Coleman, William L.
    What children need to know when parents get divorced / by William L.
Coleman.—Newly rev. ed.
        p. cm.
    Summary: Discusses the causes and results of divorce with emphasis on the
needs of children who must understand their parents' feelings as well as their own
and adjust to the changes that divorce brings about in their lives.
    1. Children of divorced parents—Juvenile literature. 2. Divorce—Juvenile
literature. 3. Parent and child—Juvenile literature. [1. Divorce. 2. Single-
parent family. 3. Parent and child.] I. Title.
HQ777.5.C64   1997
646.7'8—dc21   97–33886
ISBN 0–7642–2051–9   CIP
                                                                          AC

WILLIAM L. COLEMAN is well known for his devotional books for young people. A graduate of Washington Bible College and Grace Theological Seminary, he has written over seventy-five magazine articles. His by-line has appeared in *Christianity Today, Eternity, Campus Life,* and several other Christian magazines. As a licensed counselor he deals with many families and children as they work their way through divorce. He is available to teach seminars on the subject. Married, the father of three children, and a grandfather, he currently makes his home in Nebraska.

Suggestions for Adults

You must love a certain child very much. No doubt that's why you have picked up this book. It does not deal with the moral issues of divorce. The parents themselves must wrestle with that problem. But the child of divorce has been helpless through the ordeal. He now has parents at two addresses, and he loves them both. He is probably wondering if *anyone* really loves him. This child has been hurt in an adult world, and it isn't fair. Whether you are the child's parent or have some other close relationship, you no doubt want to spend some time in helping that child toward emotional healing. When you reach out to love this little person, you will be doing a work that is very close to the heart of God.

If you are a teacher or someone who works with children of divorce, you may not feel free to actually read this book with a particular child. But you may find here helpful resource material to use as you encourage and support her during a very painful time.

The purpose of this book is to provide a format for discussion. Many children deal with their pain by silence, so don't assume that an apparently adjusted child has no need to hear some answers or to have an opportunity to discuss the divorce. All the facts for every situation are not found here; these short chapters are meant to allow both the child and the adult to interact in a non-threatening setting—the reading of a book. Even some very emotionally-charged subjects can be broached through this neutral, objective tool. The goal is to open channels for communication.

To make this goal a little easier, I'd like to give a few suggestions on how to use this book. These are not immutable rules, so be sure you use them merely as springboards. Fit them to your own style, the particular situation, and the child with whom you are dealing.

1. As difficult as it may be for both of you, regularly spend time with the child talking about the divorce. Almost always, *the child feels he is to blame for the divorce*; therefore, the more he is able to discuss the situation, the less guilty he or she will feel. You could try spending fifteen minutes a day reading and discussing this material. Don't try to cover the whole book in just one or two sittings. The child needs time to mull over what has been read. Such medicine is best taken in short, regular doses.

2. Allow time for questions. If a certain chapter in the book covers an issue that has been raised in your discussion time, turn directly to

that section. As you read, remember that the material is focusing on problems that can overwhelm the child; she will need help, patience, and understanding in thinking it all through.

3. Suggest questions you think the child wants to ask but is reluctant to discuss. However, don't force an issue. It may take some time for the child to be able to come to grips with a particular point.

4. Tell the truth. There may be some things you would rather not say, at least for the moment, depending upon your relationship. A response such as "I'm not sure how I should answer that right now—let's discuss it again later," may be appropriate. However, do not "whitewash" the truth or attempt to paint a falsely positive picture; this will always backfire and could greatly increase his feelings of insecurity. And he may no longer trust you.

5. Don't defend either parent all the time. If a parent's behavior seems peculiar or improper, admit it. Tell the child you don't know why that person acts a certain way, then encourage her to ask that parent for an explanation.

6. After a certain subject has been covered in the book, reinforce the conclusions often. Remind the child frequently about how much God loves him. Also, remember to reassure him that this change in his life does not make him odd or strange.

When you sit and read with the child, you are saying she is very important, both to you and to God. The little one will know you care, that you love him and want to help her find some answers. May God bless you both as you journey together on this painful path.

William L. Coleman

Table of Contents

A Bright Tomorrow

It is often hard to understand divorce, especially when you're young. Things can change quickly, leaving you with confused feelings and plenty of questions.

You might not feel all the same things I did when my parents got their divorce, but I would guess that in some ways you probably will. Hopefully this book will help you get through the tough times and show you a bright tomorrow.

I want to thank the many people who were willing to share their feelings as I wrote this book.

May God give you a terrific future.

Bill Coleman

1

Children

Are Special

There is something great about being a child. Children have so many reasons to be happy.

There are things to do, places to go, people to be with.

Children are special. As you grow up, there will be many more things to enjoy. It's terrific to be a child.

Sometimes children become disappointed. That's to be expected. Every child feels sad or hurt once in a while. Maybe a pet has died or a bike has been stolen, or maybe the family has to move away.

Many children become sad because their parents get divorced. That happens very often—too often. Every year millions of parents get divorced. They decide they don't love each other and don't want to live together anymore.

You probably know several children whose parents are divorced. Those children may have found it difficult, but many have shown that it is possible to be happy again.

Children are like rubber balls. They have lots of bounce. When they get down, children manage to bounce up again.

There are too many fascinating things to do.

Children don't like to sit around and worry.

What would you like to do? What is your favorite game? Do you have a hobby or do you collect things? What is your favorite television show? What friend would you like to have over to your house?

Didn't God make an interesting world? And He made children special so they can enjoy so much of it. There are many good times ahead for children like you.

2

What Causes | Divorce?

Why do parents decide to end their marriage? Sometimes adults find it very difficult to get along with each other. They find themselves arguing a lot. Their arguments might be loud and angry. Some grown-ups may even physically fight with each other. Others argue silently and refuse to talk.

Divorce is a problem between adults. They are not happy with each other. When they decide they cannot enjoy living together, some married couples get a divorce.

It would be nice if a child could get her parents to stay together. Many children try to do this. After all, we feel best when all of our family can enjoy one another.

But children can't make their parents love each other. That is a decision two grown-ups must make.

Children can control some things. They can decide who to play with. They can decide if they like cake, candy, or vegetables. But children can't control their parents.

Divorce is not caused by children. One boy

thought his parents were getting divorced because he did not straighten up his room. That wasn't the reason. A girl thought her parents were getting divorced because she didn't put her toys away. That wasn't the reason, either.

Children do not cause divorces. Adults cause them. Children often feel sad, hurt, and confused when their parents separate. However, the divorce is not the child's fault. Children should not blame themselves for it.

A child can decide if a toy belongs in the corner or on a chair. He can pick up the toy and put it wherever he wants.

Adults are not like toys. Children cannot play with grown-ups and make them love each other.

God allows adults to make decisions for themselves. God may not always agree with the decisions, but He lets people make them. God will not *make* them do what He wants.

3

When Will It Happen?

It might help you adjust to the divorce if you know just what is happening. One of the important facts you will probably want to know is the day when the divorce becomes final. It is hard to keep wondering if the divorce has really taken place or not.

If you would like to know the day, be sure to ask your parents. It won't change anything, but it helps you know what is happening. Sometimes parents forget to tell the children. Tell them if you would like to know the exact day the divorce becomes official.

4

Even Good | Parents Get Divorced

If you don't get along with Jeff around the corner, that doesn't mean you are a bad person. It simply means that there is someone you don't get along with. It would be nice if you got along with Jeff better, but so far you don't.

Your parents are not getting along. Some divorcing parents fight and yell at each other. Another set of divorcing parents might be quiet and hardly talk. However they act, they are not getting along. That is why they are divorcing.

Even if they can't get along with each other, there is no reason why they can't get along with you. They can be concerned and loving parents and still get a divorce.

They can smile at you and help you with your homework and fix your bike and still get a divorce. Though they are divorcing each other, they are not divorcing *you*. They love you very, very much. Be sure to love them back.

Even good parents can get divorced.

5

The Secret | Question

All of us have questions we have wanted to ask someone. How can fish breathe in water? How do airplanes fly? Have you ever wondered how a television picture can travel through the air and come into your living room?

Questions are terrific. If you ask the right person, the answers can open up whole new ideas. A smart person is not someone who pretends to know all the answers. A smart person is a person who asks questions and finds out facts.

Divorce is difficult to understand. Your parents have never done this before. There are many things that might happen now. One good way to find out what is going to happen is to ask questions. Maybe your parents think you already know, so they won't bother to tell you. If you want to know something, the best thing to do is ask.

Pick a time when they are not busy. If they can sit down and take their time to answer, it will be better. Maybe now is an excellent time to ask.

There are all kinds of questions that come up:

Who will get the television set?

Who will your brother live with?

Who will you live with?

When will you see your father again?

When will you see your mother again?

Do your parents still love you?

Can you still go to your grandparents'?

Will your parents get married again?

Will you have to change schools?

Who will start the lawnmower?

Will you get new brothers and sisters?

Are you going to be poor?

The list of questions could be very long and still not include the questions you most want to ask. Be smart and ask the questions you have, even if they aren't included here.

6

Many Parents Get Divorced

Divorce sometimes makes us wonder if we have changed. Yet you still feel like everyone else because you are like everyone else. If your parents get a divorce, that doesn't make you different. You're still a nice person.

Today you will smile, laugh, get tired, and maybe you will share with another person. The children of divorced parents are just like other children.

Do you have friends whose parents are divorced? Can you think of someone at school or at church or on your block whose parents are divorced? You aren't the only one.

Children of divorced parents are short, tall, curly haired, dark skinned, freckled, or dimpled. They are like everyone around them.

You probably know some children and you don't know if their parents are divorced or not. They are like everybody else.

Talk to your friends who have divorced parents. They might be able to give you some tips that will make things go better for you.

7

Do Your

Parents Love You?

It feels good to be loved. We want to know that someone cares. That's why it is important to be held, hugged, and squeezed.

We like to have someone talk with us, play games, and read books. It feels great to sit close and be happy.

It's also good to have someone sew our clothes and cook our meals and listen to our stories. Love means someone cares.

Your parents will continue to love you after they divorce. Remember that the divorce is between your parents, not between *you* and your parents.

Divorced parents still love their children. The adults may not love each other, but their children are still very special.

Parents will likely be upset and might sound gruff and yell at their children sometimes while they are getting a divorce, but beneath the frustrations they are still concerned about their children. It's hard on *everyone* when two married people decide to stop loving each other.

Your parents aren't the only ones who love you.

Many children have grandparents, uncles, aunts, brothers, and sisters who love them. Your friends also love you, but usually they don't say things like that.

God loves you. God doesn't stop loving children because their parents get divorced. Every day, no matter what happens, God loves you, too. Nothing can change that.

"For I am convinced that nothing can ever separate us from his love" (Romans 8:38, NLT).

8

Love Your | Parents

If your parents are getting divorced, they need your love. Adults hurt inside when they get divorced. They wanted a happy marriage, but now their marriage is ending. It isn't easy for grown-ups. It's probably the biggest disappointment they have ever faced.

It's good to let your parents know you love them when they are getting divorced. You will make them feel better. Even if you don't agree with them, you should still love them.

Can you remember a time when you fell off a bike or tripped over a brick? The scrape on your knee or elbow really hurt. Maybe it bled or stung.

What happened when you went to your parents? Did they look at the wound? Did they wash it off or bandage it? Maybe they gave you a hug and showed they cared.

Today your parents hurt. You probably can't imagine how badly they feel. You can't heal them or stop their divorce. However, you could give them a hug and say you love them. They will feel better, and you probably will, too.

God still loves people when they hurt.

Children can love their parents when they hurt, too. It feels good to be hugged when you are sad.

"Let us continue to love one another...." (1 John 4:7, NLT).

9

Who Will | Leave?

Divorce means someone will move out of your home. Either your mother or father is going to live in another house or apartment.

Sometimes this means the children will move. In some cases one child might live with the mother and another with the father.

Where will you live after the divorce? You will feel better when you find out. If no one has told you where you will live, you can ask.

In most families the father moves away because of the divorce. However, this is not always true. Mother might be the one to leave.

Mothers often stay with the children because they usually have more practice taking care of children. Mothers usually know more about cooking, ironing, cleaning, and curling hair.

The father might leave. That will hurt. However, that does not mean your father does not love you. Divorce results in some things that hurt.

10

Get Back Together?

Imagine that you could wish or pray, and your parents would end their divorce. That would be exciting. It would be nice if you could just talk to them and patch everything up.

This is very unlikely to happen. If your parents are divorced, they are not planning to ever live together again. Divorce means the marriage is over.

Parents almost never undo a divorce. If a leaf dies and falls to the ground, it does not later get up and climb back on the tree. If you cut a rope, it does not come back together again.

You will not be two years old again. That age is over. Your parents do not want to be married to each other again. They consider the marriage as having ended.

From now on you will have two parents who are not married to each other. At the same time, they will still be concerned about _you_, and they will still be your parents.

11

The Unhappy Facts

You expect a book to be honest with you. Divorce is hard enough; you don't need a book to tell you a bunch of fairy tales. Some bad things could happen and you need to know. Throughout this book more of these hard facts will be discussed.

Sometimes the parent who moved out begins to drift farther and farther away. Some will promise to see their children often and don't. We hope this isn't true for you, but it's possible. Some parents come around less and less, and some never visit.

If the parent who moves out doesn't come to see you, there isn't much you can do. That might hurt, but it is a fact, though an unhappy one.

If it happens that way, it *isn't* your fault. Unfortunately, some parents just can't face seeing their children and being reminded of the marriage that is over. There is no reason to blame yourself.

Let your parent know that you want him to come to see you. Let her know how much you love her. Let him know that you hope he will remain the kind of good parent who likes to be with you.

These are the facts, but it will not always be exactly the same for each family of divorce.

12

Talk To

When people are going through difficult times, they often need someone to talk to. They need someone who will listen to how they feel. Adults need to talk and so do children.

Other people can help us understand what is happening. They can often answer our questions and explain things that might worry us. Sometimes we just need someone to listen. It's fun to talk to people and it makes us feel better.

Who can you talk to? It has to be a nice person, someone you like. Sometimes it needs to be a child your age, and at other times it needs to be an older person.

Who would you like to talk to? Your parents? Your teacher? A grandparent? Another relative? A minister? A counselor? A Sunday school teacher? A neighbor you have known for a long time? People can be a big help when you need them.

Another person you might enjoy talking to is God. He would like to hear how you feel. God watches over His children and cares about them.

Don't worry about the words you use. We can

talk to God the same way we speak to our friends. Tell Him exactly how you feel. Ask Him to help you while your parents separate.

You won't need to make an appointment. God will listen while you are walking, biking, climbing a tree, lying in bed, or taking a bath.

Children often feel much better after talking to God about their problems.

13

Some Tough Words

Janis and Chris were quietly playing a game when suddenly things began to change. They were soon arguing and pushing. Janis became so upset she finally yelled at Chris, "I never have liked you!"

When we feel hurt or disappointed, we often say harsh things. We might want to say something cruel to make a person feel bad.

That can happen when two people are getting divorced. A parent feels hurt inside, and that might result in saying some mean things about the other parent.

You understand that. When people are upset they also get excited.

Neither of your parents is perfect. It's true that they have done some things wrong. All of us do. However, not all of the things that are said are really meant.

One parent might say some things about the other parent and later wish they hadn't. Remember that both your parents are trying to protect themselves from any more hurt. Everybody does that at some time.

When your parent calms down, he might feel differently. Avoid arguing with your parents if they are upset—it will only make things worse.

14

Children | Smile Again!

When we are sad, everything seems gloomy. Our face drops, our lower lip might shake, and we might cry. Sadness makes us feel bad inside.

It would be nice if we could feel good all the time, but we can't. Disappointments are part of life. We will be sad a number of times as we grow up.

Everyone is sad at some time or another!

The good thing about sadness is that it is meant to go away. Happiness is meant to come back and push the disappointment out. Parents and children will smile again, even after a divorce.

Children may wish their parents were back together, but they learn to be happy again. Children will laugh, play, sing, run, and enjoy life.

God has made us in a wonderful way. Happiness keeps coming back.

15

Aches and | Pains

Your body is in tune with your head and your feelings. When we worry, our body often begins to do strange things. If we are afraid, our stomach might begin to feel sick. When we are confused, we could start to get headaches.

When your parents are getting divorced, you may feel sick. Divorce is usually one of the hardest things anyone goes through. Don't be surprised if sometimes you don't feel like doing anything.

Fortunately, this is the kind of illness that will go away. You might not even get it at all.

You don't know what is going to happen next. You aren't sure what caused the divorce. You have questions about tomorrow, about your home, about your mother and father, about money, about love, about your brothers and sisters and grandparents. You are bothered about things you don't even understand. It's truly enough to make a person sick.

Two things could start to make you feel better: time and answers. As time goes on, many cloudy questions will become clear. As questions are answered, life begins to settle down.

If you are feeling physically ill about the divorce, you probably will begin to feel better soon.

16

How Do

You Feel?

What did you feel like when your parents decided to get divorced? Were you surprised? Did you feel hurt inside? Did it make you sad? Did you feel confused? Have you had some idea for a while that things were not going well between your parents?

All of us have our own feelings. That's normal. Some children might even feel glad that their parents are separating because then their arguing and fighting will stop.

However you feel is fine. Don't be afraid or ashamed about your feelings.

Some children would like to cry because of the divorce. If you would like to cry, it would be all right. After you cry for a while, you will probably feel a little better.

Sometimes Jesus felt very sad and He wanted to cry. He was strong but He still cried. If you feel like crying sometimes, that is just fine.

17

Are You

Glad?

There are some children who are glad that their parents are getting divorced. They have listened to their parents argue. Some have seen them hit each other. They have seen fear, anger, confusion, and tears on the faces of their parents. Some of these children are relieved to see their parents separate.

They would like to have their parents happy together, but it did not happen. After a long time of misery, they are glad to see the divorce.

It's all right to feel that way. We can't all feel the same. You might want your parents back together but not with things the way they were.

If you aren't sad about the divorce, you don't have to pretend you are. If you are confused, sort of glad and sort of sad, that's all right, too.

The more important thing is to be honest about how you feel. Kind but honest. Talk to people about how you feel.

How do you feel about the divorce?

18

Getting | Angry

Does divorce make you angry? Do you ever get just good and mad because your parents don't live together anymore? Many children do feel angry about it. It is not unusual if you react this way.

But many kids in this situation don't know what to do about their anger. All they know is that they are confused, hurt, and frustrated. It is easy to blame the two people you love the most for these feelings. Some children are angry at their parents and stay angry their whole lifetime.

It's all right to feel angry. But try to direct your angry thoughts at the problems that *caused* the divorce—not at your parents. This will be very hard to do and it takes practice, but you will eventually feel much better inside if you can do this.

Some things in life don't seem fair. It isn't fair to have a house burn down. It isn't fair for a dog to get hit by a car.

Other things in life are neither fair nor right. It isn't fair or right for someone to steal your bike. It isn't fair or right for two parents to stop loving each other and living together. But it happens.

It's okay to be angry with things in life that are

wrong. You can be angry with the divorce and its destructive effect on people's lives.

But don't stay angry. There is too much life to enjoy, too much fun to be had, too many good things to do. You will miss many of these if you hang on to your anger.

If anger fills your mind too long, it begins to hurt you. After you are finished being angry, you can start to get the best out of life. There were wrong situations in life that angered Jesus, but He didn't stay angry.

19

Are You Being Punished?

Some children wonder if God is punishing them by having their parents get a divorce. Maybe a kid has stolen something, lied, or used some terrible language—maybe something even worse.

The child believes very strongly in God, and now he wonders if God is getting even. Don't worry. God is not like that. But if you have ever thought this, don't be surprised. Many children (and adults) have asked themselves the same thing.

God loves you very much. He looks for ways to help you.

He is caring. He is understanding. He is patient. He is forgiving. He is helpful. God would not split your family because *you* don't make your bed. God would not separate your parents because *you* cheated on your homework. You are not being punished. The divorce is not your fault.

Love. Kindness. Encouragement. Cheerfulness. God enjoys spreading these around.

20

What Becomes of the Children?

What kind of adults do the children of divorce become? Are they different from other children? No.

They become flight attendants.
They become governors.
They become missionaries.
They become presidents.
They become police officers.
They become teachers.
They become doctors.
They become nurses.
They become soldiers.
They become musicians.
They become husbands.
They become wives.
They become ministers.
They become secretaries.

Divorce hurts, but it doesn't have to stop us from becoming whatever we would like to be. For some children it makes them wiser sooner. For others it helps them to be careful as they make decisions.

Your future is just as bright as you care to make

it. Your dreams for tomorrow can come true.

The children of divorced parents are like everyone else. They get their sleeves in the gravy. They win the fifty-yard dash. They lose their contact lenses. They are good spellers. They forget where they left their lunches. They are chosen president of the class.

And very often they grow up to be extremely happy.

21

Where Is
God?

Do you ever wonder why God hasn't done something about this divorce? That's a fair question. Why didn't God change your parents' hearts or make them love each other more?

Maybe you prayed and asked God to change the situation, but the divorce still happened. That is confusing. By now you might even be a little disappointed with God.

One of the reasons God doesn't stop divorce is that He wants us to love each other because we choose to. He wants a mother to *choose* to love a father. He wants a father to *choose* to love a mother.

He could "zap" people and make them love each other, but God doesn't work that way. To "zap" people would make them into robots. That type of love is not real.

God leaves it up to us. He hopes that we will keep loving each other, but He will not make us do it. He puts love in our hearts and hopes we will use it, but God doesn't force us to love if we do not want to.

When your parents got divorced, God cared

very much. Do you think He is more disappointed and hurt by the divorce than you? He could be.

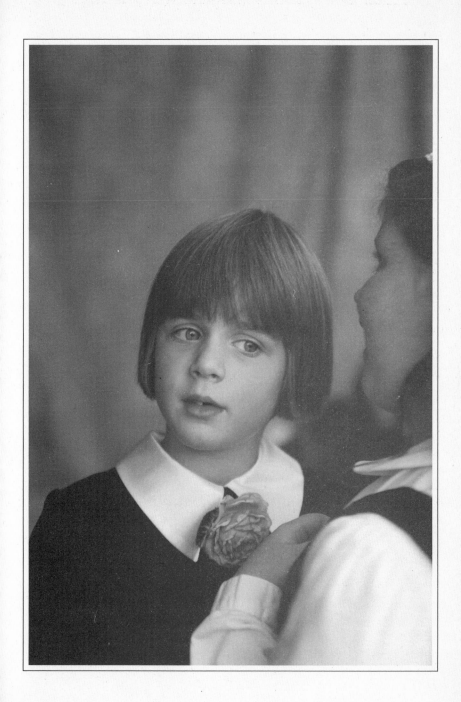

22

Who Will Pay for the Pizza?

It takes money to buy many of the things you are used to having. Clothes, shoes, trips, movies, and thick, chewy pizza all cost money. Are these things going to change after the divorce? Will life be harder? Are you going to be poor?

There are added expenses in getting a divorce. Instead of one place to live, there now must be two. How much will this change the way you live?

It's important to know the facts. I've said this before; good information helps erase fears and allows us to be prepared for the future.

Most of us could live on less if we had to. A small dip in income might not be too painful. However, it helps a great deal if you know what to expect.

Think about the questions you would like to ask. Will you be able to go to camp? What about vacations? And who will pay for the pizza?

Don't expect to hear the exact number of dollars, but it might make you feel better if you knew the facts about any changes in how you will live.

23

Make | Popcorn!

Sandy's best friend, Lorrie, moved to another city. Sandy was convinced it was the saddest day of her life. She wondered if she could ever be happy again.

Soon Sandy decided to accept the facts. Lorrie would not, could not, move back. She was gone. If Sandy sulked for two hours, two weeks, or two years, nothing was going to change.

That's when Sandy decided to get up, brush her hair, call another friend, and enjoy life. If she stayed sad too long, she was going to miss out on too much.

Divorce is a bad deal. It would be better if everyone could live happily ever after. But many don't. And people get hurt.

There is no sense wasting all our tomorrows crying over what we can't change. Maybe it's time to get up, call a friend, and make popcorn.

You are going to laugh again. You are going to make funny faces and play soccer. You are going to ride a sled and swim. It's still a fascinating world.

Tomorrow or the next day you might be with

some friends and laugh until your sides ache. Life is still terrific.

24

Parents | Cry, Too

We aren't used to seeing adults cry. They are supposed to be big and tough. No matter what happens, we expect parents to be as strong as the walls of our house. It's often a surprise when we see one of them crying.

In some ways we are all alike. In some ways parents are grown-up children. In some ways children are small adults. All of us have feelings. All of us are a little bit afraid. All of us like to be loved. All of us like to laugh. No one wants to be hurt.

Divorce means your parents are losing someone they used to love very much. Maybe they *still* love that one. That person will be gone. The marriage will now be dead.

No matter what has happened to cause the divorce, it is going to be hard. Your mother and father will both feel drained and tired and maybe disappointed.

Don't be surprised if they cry. That's okay. It's even good for them. They will be all right later. Maybe soon you will be laughing with them again.

Stay close. It's nice to be loved when you are crying.

"*A time to cry ...*" (Ecclesiastes 3:4, NLT).

25

Touch Your | Family

Our girl, June, dislocated her shoulder when she was in grade school. She was in the hospital for about five hours and had a great deal of pain.

Afterward she said the most helpful part was when people touched her. The doctor and nurse stood by the bed and explained what they were going to do. As they talked to June they touched her good arm. Just the touching calmed her down and made her feel like everything would be all right.

Members of your family will feel pain because of the divorce. It might make them feel better if you touch them. Hug them. Place your hands on their shoulders. Touching does a lot to say "I care" or "I love you."

Your parents could use a warm squeeze. Your grandparents might appreciate it if you hold their hands. Even a brother or sister would enjoy the feel of your arm around a shoulder.

Divorce can be cold. Often divorce makes everyone want to stay away from one another. Everyone would probably appreciate the warmth of your touch.

26

some | Teasing

Children often tease one another. All of us have done it, and we have had it done to us. We have called each other names and have been called a few.

Don't be too surprised if some of your friends tease you about the divorce. Most children probably won't even mention it. A few will be very understanding. Others like to tease anyone about anything.

Teasing is part of life, and there isn't much we can do about it. But it probably won't last long. Maybe no one will tease you at all.

You might just as well get it over with. Tell a couple of your friends about the divorce. Soon many people will know. When you tell your friends about it, you don't need to explain everything. There could be some facts you would like to keep secret. It's entirely up to you.

You might feel better after you tell someone. That way you won't have to carry the burden of it by yourself.

27

Brothers | and Sisters

How many people are in your family? Sometimes all the children stay together after a divorce. At other times some live with one parent and some live with another.

Has your family decided where everyone will live? How do you feel about that? Will you live far apart? When will you see each other again?

If you have brothers and sisters, the change could be hard for them, too. An older child might react one way and a younger child might react entirely differently.

It helps if brothers and sisters talk to each other about divorce. One can explain something the other one doesn't understand. Maybe someone has an idea that is totally wrong. Talking to a person in the same situation could be a big help.

Often it is easy to talk to a brother or sister. You might make each other feel much better. If there is something that none of you know, you can find out together.

28

A Name | Game

Divorces and remarriages present confusing problems with people's names. Often you meet a child who has a different name than his parents. It takes a little explaining.

There are several things that could happen to people's names. Take a look at some of the possibilities and ask your parents which one might take place. They may not know for sure, but maybe they have some ideas for you to think about.

Your father's name will stay the same. If you live with him, your name will not change.

Your mother could keep her present name. No change for you.

Your mother could take back her maiden name (the one she had before she married your father). Your name still would not need to change.

Your name would change if your mother changes hers and you want to change yours to match hers.

Your name would change if your mother remarried and your stepfather adopted you.

That sounds confusing. Ask your parents

if your name will change. (They might not know yet.)

29

Parents Make Mistakes, Too

When you were little, you may have thought your parents were always right. It seemed that they could do anything. They knew everything and could fix anything. If you needed a pair of socks, all you had to do was ask your mother; she would find a pair someplace.

As you get older, you discover that parents can make mistakes. They forget things. They don't always have a good answer. You find out your parents can be wrong. It's an important part of growing up.

More than once your parents may disappoint you. They may say, "I'll see you next Tuesday." But they could forget and not get there. Maybe a birthday or other special day will pass and your parent might forget it.

It sometimes helps to remind a parent. It also helps to ask a parent what happened. They may have a good explanation. That will make you feel better.

Most important, we need to learn to forgive our parents when they make mistakes. They have often forgiven the mistakes we made.

Forgive your parents! It's a loving thing to do. That must be why God does it so often for us.

"Instead, be kind to each other, tenderhearted, forgiving one another, just as God has forgiven you because you belong to Christ" (Ephesians 4:32, NLT).

30

Time Together

When Allen lost one of his in-line skates, he was especially sad. However, the lost skate made Allen learn to ride a bike. It hurts to lose something, but often something else good comes from it.

Even divorce can have some good parts. Divorce does not mean that God cannot still bring about some good things for you. Some parents spend more time with their children after a divorce than before. That might not happen to you, but it could. Sometimes divorce makes parents realize how much they love their children.

Don't wait around for this to happen. If you can't have your two parents together, try to get them one at a time.

Where would you like to go and what would you like to do? How does the zoo sound? What about a picnic or flying kites? Have you ever been to a ball game or gone fishing?

Use your imagination. (Try not to make it too hard or expensive.) Tell your parent what you would like to do with him or her.

If you can't have your parents together, enjoy

them one at a time.
"A time for loving ..." (Ecclesiastes 3:8, NLT).

31

Praying for | Parents

When you love your parents, there are some very nice things you can do for them. One of the most caring things we can do is to pray for our parents. Maybe at night, just before you go to sleep, talk to God about your mother and father.

Pray for the parent you live with and see every day. Pray that parent will have good health and know what decisions to make about your lives together. Thank God for the daily love He shows.

Pray for the parent you can't see tonight. Ask God to remind that one of your love, and ask God to show His love.

Ask God to give the parent you are not with a wide smile and good health. Ask that God will keep him or her safely through the day.

There is a lot we will not understand about a divorce. However, we do know how loving it is to pray for one another.

32

Love Has | Long Arms

My children have an aunt who lives many miles away. They don't get to see one another often, but they love each other very much. Love has long arms. It can reach across the miles and care for people who live in other places.

One of your parents will leave your home and live someplace else. You won't get to see each other as often, but that won't stop you from loving each other. Many children continue to love both parents equally.

Your parents might not love each other anymore, but that doesn't have to change the way you feel. If you live with one parent, it doesn't mean you need to love the other parent any differently.

The parent you live with will do many more things for you, helping you with many things in your daily life—homework, cleaning, and talking to you often. However, you can still love the parent who has moved. Love has long arms.

"Dear friends, let us practice loving each other, for love comes from God..." (1 John 4:7, NLT).

33

Here Comes | Santa Claus

Have you ever hurt someone and then tried to give him something so he wouldn't cry? Maybe you gave him a piece of candy or a toy.

Don't be surprised if one of your parents tries to do this. Maybe both of them will. They might want to buy you presents or take you someplace special. A parent knows that you are hurt and might be trying to make you feel better.

The parent also might be trying to prove he or she is not bad. Your parents want you to think they are nice.

It's okay if a parent wants to play Santa Claus. All of us enjoy getting presents.

Later the presents might come less often. That's okay, too.

The parent who gives presents and the parent who doesn't give presents might both love you exactly the same. Love usually shows itself best when someone cares, helps, listens, shares, and spends time with you.

If a parent wants to play Santa Claus, you should be thankful for the gifts. But we know that love can also be shown without presents.

34

Just | Dreaming

What are the things you like to pretend about? Do you ever imagine yourself as a queen with long, fluffy pink dresses? Do you ever pretend you caught a pass for the winning touchdown while thousands of excited fans screamed? Pretending and dreaming are fun for most of us.

Dreaming comes in handy, especially if things are going tough. We can imagine ourselves in another place, at another time, when things are going great.

Don't be surprised if you find yourself day-dreaming once in a while because of the divorce. The parent you stay with will have to have house rules. Sometimes that parent may be low on money, some days possibly even short tempered and grouchy.

When that happens you might dream that your other parent would not be like that. It is easy to pretend that the parent you do not live with would treat you much better.

Usually that is just a dream and is not based on fact.

If you lived with your other parent, that parent

would have rules, too. The rules might be different, but they would still be there. Someday that one would also be tired and get fussy, too. Most likely every parent will have days when there isn't much money.

Besides, your other parent might have some rules this parent does not have.

When people live together they must have rules. Who will vacuum the floor? Who will clean out the refrigerator? Who is going to cook?

It is easy to dream that it would be easier at your other parent's home, but it might be much the same. The rules could be different, but there would still be rules. Rules are helpful.

35

A Gift
of Time

It's fun to do things with our parents. Maybe you like to wrestle on the floor or learn to cook together. Many children like to play catch, shoot baskets, or read with a parent.

One of the best things a parent gives a child is the gift of time. It doesn't matter so much what you do; the most important part is that you spend time together. It feels great just to touch your father's hand or hear your mother's voice. It's terrific to know they want to spend time with you.

When someone spends time with you, he is saying he cares about you. Giving your time to someone is like giving love.

If we enjoy someone, we enjoy having him around.

With one parent out of the house, time will become more important. It won't be as easy to get together. Both of you will have to make time. You can't meet just when it's easy. You and your parent will have to work harder to make sure you get together.

The extra effort is worth it. You might have to give up something else so you can do things. Your mother or father will have to make it happen, too.

It might be best to tell your parents you want to spend time with each of them. They probably both want to spend time with you, too. Maybe your parent who is away is wondering how you feel. Don't make a guessing game out of this. Tell him or her exactly how you feel about getting together.

Get the facts. When will you meet? Will your parent come to you or will you go to him or her? Time is a fantastic gift. Make sure you give it to each other.

36

Picking | Sides

It's hard to be a judge. He goes to school for years. When he hears a case, a judge tries to weigh all the evidence and listen to everyone. And it still might be hard to decide who is right and who is wrong.

Trying to judge people in your own family is more difficult than working in a court. For one thing, we don't have all the evidence. We can't be sure what has gone on. For another thing, we love the people involved. That makes it twice as hard to blame someone.

When your parents get divorced, you don't have to judge who was right and who was wrong. Maybe one parent will try to get you to pick sides against another parent. That isn't fair. Divorce is an adult problem. It isn't for children to decide who is at fault.

As far as possible, try to stay in the middle. Give each parent as much love as you can. Both of them need it.

You may even have to tell your parents that you don't like to be asked to judge. Tell them it makes you very confused and hurt to pick sides. They may not even realize they are doing it.

37

Back | to Happy

The sun is going to shine again. How soon it will happen is partly up to you. There is nothing we can do about yesterday, but there is so much we can do about today.

What are some of the things you enjoy the most? Do you like to play basketball, swim, go camping, eat cotton candy, ride go-carts, spend the night with a friend, or run with your dog? There are so many terrific things to do. It's time to get back to being happy.

Nothing will completely heal the pain of divorce. There is no sense in pretending that everything is great. But sitting around and moping will only make it worse.

Activity has a healing medicine all its own. You *will* be happy again. You may as well make it as soon as you can. Don't wait another day to begin to go back to being happy. See if you can take your first steps today.

38

You Will Never

Be a Jet Plane

When you were younger, did you ever pretend to be an airplane? Maybe you spread out your arms, made noises like an engine, and "flew" around the backyard.

No matter how often you did this or how high you jumped, you never became a jet plane. Some things are impossible even if you pretend as hard as you can.

You are a child, and until you grow up you will stay a child.

The children of divorce are sometimes asked to be something else. A child might think she has to become a mother to her younger brother or sister. Her own mother has either gotten a job or moved to another house. The child thinks she has to take her mother's place.

But she is a child. And children cannot be mothers or jet planes.

A boy might feel the same way. He could start to act like a father because his father is gone.

A boy can't be a father—or a jet plane. He is still a child. And this is as it should be.

Many times a child of divorced parents has to

take more responsibility. There are often extra jobs to do. You might have to help cook, watch other children, or vacuum the carpet.

In some ways the children of divorce grow up faster than others. They see a little more trouble and they have to take care of themselves more.

However, they are still children. They cannot be a mother or a father. They must stay children until they are older.

39

If You | Lose a Hand

Suppose a girl was in a car accident and had to have her left hand removed. She probably never thought about her hands much before. From now on she will probably think much more about her right hand. What would happen if she lost that hand, too?

Most of us do not think about losing our parents. However, when one of them moves out, it makes us wonder about a lot of things.

Have you ever wondered what will happen if the other parent leaves, too? This question should be asked. The answer will make you feel much better.

You might want to ask your parent what would happen to you if he or she should leave, too.

Maybe the answer will be that the parent you are with never expects to leave. That answer would feel good. But what if he or she got sick and had to be in the hospital? What would happen?

Will you go to stay with an uncle or an aunt or a grandparent? Will you go to stay with your other parent?

These things do not happen to most of us. You

might keep living with the one parent. Still, it's nice to know "what if" answers.

Some people wonder and worry, but they never ask. Since your life is being changed by divorce, it would be good if you had some answers.

When we know the facts, it usually makes us feel better.

40

Tell Me | Again

Do you have any songs you enjoy hearing over and over again? Even though you know the words, it's fun to hear them one more time.

There are many things to learn about divorce. Often we forget and need to be told again. That is part of learning.

Some things we remember, but it feels good to hear them from someone else one more time. The more time you spend talking about the divorce, the better you will probably feel.

Later, more questions will occur to you, and you will want to ask them. Just ten or fifteen minutes a day could make it go easier.

You might want to hear again that your parents love you. You might like to be reminded that it isn't your fault. Maybe you want to hear once more about the happiness ahead.

Read together. Ask questions. Rehearse the facts as you would a play. It feels good to be told again.

41

A New | Person

Once the changes in a divorce begin, it is difficult to tell which change will come next. Some children find themselves living in a new home, a new neighborhood, living with a different amount of money and meeting new people.

Some of these new things can be exciting. Others are great disappointments and you wish they wouldn't happen. But you can expect change as a normal part of divorce.

One of the biggest changes might be new people coming into your life. It's possible that your mother or your father will meet someone else who becomes special in his or her life. Maybe both of them will.

Can you imagine your father or mother dating someone else? That might seem strange at first. It may even seem rather mean to you.

Many children will resent a new person coming into their parents' lives. Some will be able to accept it as a normal part of divorce.

It is not weird to feel resentful toward the person who may become special in a parent's life. It may take some time to get used to another person being special to your parent. Talk with your parents about this. Ask them to give you time. Friendships cannot be forced—they must be developed.

In the meantime, it will help you and your parent if you can be friendly and kind toward this new person. Be courteous and accepting. Talk with the person and show an interest.

Friendliness and love always make change go better.

"There are three things that remain—faith, hope, and love—and the greatest of these is love" (1 Corinthians 13:13, NLT).

42

Future | Family

It would be great if someone could tell you what the future will be like. Will you always live in the town where you are now? Maybe you will move to a better, more exciting place. Part of what makes tomorrow interesting is the changes that happen.

One of the changes that often comes after divorce is that a parent might remarry. Maybe both parents will marry. Maybe you don't want that now, but it could happen.

A new parent is usually called a stepparent. Many stepparents are very wonderful people. They can be caring, loving, and sharing.

Maybe no one has mentioned getting married. Maybe there are no plans to get a stepparent. However, you probably would like to know if it is likely to happen. That would be a good question to ask your parents.

The more you know, the better you can feel about the future. If you are going to have a step-parent, you will want to start adjusting to the idea as soon as possible.

To help you adjust, you need to understand

some facts about this situation.

First, it is not your responsibility or place to judge whether or not your parent *should* remarry. Divorce was your parents' decision; remarriage is your parents' decision. It is their choice to make—you cannot make the choice for them.

Second, you *can* express to your parents how you feel. It would be best to talk alone to your parents about it. Remember to ask them to give you time to adjust and not to force you to like this new person. Help them realize the way you are feeling—you are only human. You can also pray about it. God is concerned about this relationship, too.

Third, be assured that no one will be able to *replace* your own parents. The stepparent won't take the place of your mom or dad but will be an *additional* parent. Your relationship with your folks is not meant to change by this.

Fourth, though your stepparent cannot replace your parent, it is possible to become very close to him or her. It may take time and special effort, but it is important to you and to your family that you adjust. Don't become resentful. Make the best of your new family situation.

43

Do *You* Want to Get Married?

It's too early to know if *you* are going to get married, but it isn't too early to be told some facts. Your parents are divorced. They decided they did not want to live together any longer. But many people stay married to one person all of their lives. Have you heard of a couple who has been married for fifty years or more?

Divorce is hard. It makes some people never want to get married. But divorce doesn't happen to everyone. Many people choose to stay in love and remain married for many years.

When you get old enough to think about marriage, you will have learned a great deal. You will see marriages that are very happy. You have seen a marriage that wasn't happy.

Your own marriage could be great. You could be married to the same person all your life and really be happy.

Your whole future is spread out ahead of you like a long, bright ribbon of highway. There will no doubt be some other difficult times ahead, but Jesus himself wants to help you through them and give you a wonderful life.

"I pray that Christ will be more and more at home in your hearts, living within you as you trust in him. May your roots go down deep into the soil of God's marvelous love; and may you be able to feel and understand, as all God's children should, how long, how wide, how deep, and how high his love really is..." (Ephesians 3:17-19, NLT).